CRaZy NaTuRe™

Animals with Armor

Marie Racanelli

PowerKiDS press™

New York

To Ellen Clark and Paul Violi

Published in 2010 by The Rosen Publishing Group, Inc.
29 East 21st Street, New York, NY 10010

First Edition

Editor: Joanne Randolph
Book Design: Greg Tucker
Photo Researcher: Jessica Gerweck

Photo Credits: Cover © Photoshot/age fotostock; pp. 5, 7, 11, 12–13, 19, 21 Shutterstock.com; p. 9 Andy Rouse/ Getty Images; p. 15 © www.iStockphoto.com/Greg Brzezinski; p. 17 © James L. Amos/Peter Arnold, Inc.

Library of Congress Cataloging-in-Publication Data

Racanelli, Marie.
  Animals with armor / Marie Racanelli. — 1st ed.
      p. cm. — (Crazy nature)
  Includes index.
  ISBN 978-1-4358-9386-3 (library binding) — ISBN 978-1-4358-9864-6 (pbk.) — ISBN 978-1-4358-9865-3 (6-pack)
  1. Armored animals—Juvenile literature. I. Title.
  QL940.R33 2010
  591.47'7—dc22
                                2009036527

Manufactured in the United States of America

CPSIA Compliance Information: Batch #WW10PK: For Further Information contact Rosen Publishing, New York, New York at 1-800-237-9932

Contents

What Is Animal Armor?   4

Lots of Different Armored Animals   6

Turtles and Tortoises   8

Scaly Armor   10

Crazy Armor Facts!   13

Armadillos and Armored Mammals   14

Armored Bugs   16

Snails!   18

Underwater Armor   20

Why Is Armor So Important?   22

Glossary   23

Index   24

Web Sites   24

What Is Animal Armor?

Animals all over the world have different coverings on their bodies. Some animals have fur. Others animals have feathers. Some kinds of animals have strong, hard coverings. All these coverings help the animals live in their **habitats**. A bear's fur keeps it warm and dry in its home. A bluejay's feathers help it fly and find a mate. Why might an animal need a hard, strong covering?

A long time ago, knights wore heavy **armor** to **protect** themselves before going into battle. Some animals are born with special coverings that are like that armor, such as hard scales, shells, and thick skin. Let's take a closer look at animals with armor.

Hermit crabs, such as the one shown here, use old shells from other sea animals to keep their bodies safe. As they grow, they move into bigger shells.

Lots of Different Armored Animals

There are many animals that have developed armor on their bodies as a **defense** against **predators**. You can find them all over the world.

Some animals, like snails and turtles, carry hard shells on their backs. Lobsters and crabs have shells, too. Crocodiles and alligators are covered in thick, bony plates and scales. Hippos do not have scales or shells, but they have skin that is so thick that it can be nearly **impenetrable** to a predator's bite. These animals are so well protected that you might say it is as if they had their own built-in bodyguards!

Hippos may look soft and slow moving, but they are not cuddly animals. Hippos will fight any animal that does not belong in their space.

Turtles and Tortoises

When you think of animals with shells, you might think of turtles and tortoises. Turtles live in or near water. Tortoises live mostly on land. Turtles and tortoises cannot crawl out of their shells. Their bodies are attached to these hard coverings. Their shells are made of bone that is covered in thick scales, called **scutes**. The top of the shell is known as the carapace.

Some turtles and tortoises can pull their heads and legs into the shell when they are in danger. Others just turn their heads to the side and tuck them under the edge of the shell.

These Galápagos giant tortoises sit in a muddy pond to cool off. The spines and ribs of turtles and tortoises are actually part of their shells.

Scaly Armor

Some animals, such as alligators and crocodiles, are kept safe by rows of thick, hard scales. Some of these scales may have points or ridges on them. Not only do crocodiles and alligators have thick skin, but they also have bony pieces of armor under their skin. It is no wonder that adult alligators and crocodiles have very few predators!

Lizards and snakes have tough scales, too. The spiny-tailed lizard, which lives in Africa, has a special piece of armor on its hide. It has large, pointed scales on its thick tail. It swings its tail at enemies to keep them away.

You can see the scales that cover this crocodile's body. The scales are smaller on the legs and sides, and they are larger along the back and tail.

Crazy Armor Facts!

1. The hippo's thick skin acts like armor. It keeps the hippo safe from biting insects as well as the much bigger bites of crocodiles and lions that are looking for dinner.

2. The skin of a hippo gives off a reddish watery matter that kills illness-causing **bacteria**. This matter also acts as a sunscreen to protect the hippo's skin from the strong sun in its African home.

3. If a scallop, a kind of shellfish, senses danger approaching, it keeps its shell tightly closed so that its enemy cannot hurt its soft body.

4. The largest lobster ever found weighed about 44 pounds (20 kg). Scientists guess that it was about 100 years old!

5. Water snails have thicker shells than land snails. The water helps the snails carry the weight of their shells.

6. A giant clam can have a shell that is about 4 feet (1 m) wide!

7. One kind of South American armadillo, called the three-banded armadillo, can completely curl up into a ball to keep itself safe. It is the only armadillo that can do this.

8. A pill millipede can curl up into a ball if it is attacked. Enemies find the ball hard to pull open, so they leave it alone.

Armadillos and Armored Mammals

Have you ever seen an armadillo? An armadillo is a **mammal** that has a very hard covering. Its name means "little armored one." There are about 20 different kinds of armadillos. Some are so small they fit in the palm of your hand. Others can be as big as a large cat. Their armor is made up of bony plates that are covered by scutes.

A pangolin is another armored mammal. It has large, bony plates all over its body. The plates make it look a bit like a really big, walking pinecone! It lives in Africa and Asia. To escape danger, it curls up into a ball.

This armadillo is called the yellow or six-banded armadillo, and it lives in South America. It has six to eight moveable bands along its plated back.

Armored Bugs

Your skeleton is on the inside of your body. It is made of bone and helps hold up your body. It grows along with you. Insects, spiders, and some other animals have **exoskeletons**, which support their bodies from the outside. They do not have skeletons inside their bodies. Exoskeletons are generally made up of **flexible** skin and hard plates. These plates work like armor and keep the animals safe.

Some insects have sharp, tough spikes sticking out of their legs, too. This gives them extra protection. They may also have hairs or scales, as on a butterfly's wings.

In order to grow, insects must molt, or shed, their exoskeletons. Here a cicada is climbing out of its old, smaller shell.

Snails!

Snails are another kind of armored animal. Snails are **gastropods**, which are part of the soft-bodied mollusk, or shellfish, family. Not all snails live in the ocean, though. Many kinds of snails may even live in your garden.

Did you know that when a snail breaks out of its egg, it eats the shell? It eats most of it, leaving just a small piece. This small piece of shell grows larger as the snail grows larger. The hard shell grows into a spiral shape, and it protects the soft body of the snail. Snails are attached to their shells and cannot ever leave them.

This land snail is related to sea snails, freshwater snails, and slugs. Its shell protects it from birds and other dangers.

Underwater Armor

Sea animals also need to find ways to be safe. It is not surprising, then, to find armored animals, such as crabs and lobsters, in the water. Oysters, clams, and many other sea animals have shells, too.

A crab is completely covered by a hard shell. The shell even covers its legs. When it gets too big for its shell, it will **molt**. This means the crab will shed its old shell and grow a new one. A hermit crab is not a true crab. Its shell is softer than the shell of a regular crab and so it uses another animal's shell to stay safe. As it grows, it needs to find bigger shells in which to live.

A lobster, such as this tropical lobster, has a tough outer shell and ten legs. As it gets bigger, it molts and then eats its old shell.

Why Is Armor So Important?

Animals have **adapted** in remarkable ways in order to keep themselves safe from their enemies. Some animals are poisonous or have sharp teeth and claws to keep them safe. Others have colors or markings on their bodies that help them hide.

Armor is just another crazy way that some animals keep themselves safe. Armor makes it hard for predators to bite and eat an animal. It also keeps insects from biting the animal and causing illness. Armor can also be useful if an animal lives in a place with lots of branches, thorns, or rocks that could hurt its body. Armor is important in keeping many animals alive and healthy!

Glossary

adapted (uh-DAPT-ed) Changed to fit requirements.

armor (AR-mer) A hard cover over something that keeps it safe.

bacteria (bak-TIR-ee-uh) Tiny living things that cannot be seen with the eye alone. Some bacteria cause illness or rotting, but others are helpful.

defense (dih-FENTS) Something a living thing does that helps keep it safe.

exoskeletons (ek-soh-SKEH-leh-tunz) Hard coverings on the outside of animals' bodies that hold and guard the soft insides.

gastropods (GAS-truh-podz) Kinds of soft-bodied mollusks, or shellfish, that have heads and single feet. The name means "belly footed."

habitats (HA-beh-tats) Places where animals or plants naturally live.

impenetrable (im-PEH-neh-truh-bel) Impossible to get in or through.

mammal (MA-mul) A warm-blooded animal that has a backbone and hair, breathes air, and feeds milk to its young.

molt (MOHLT) To shed hair, feathers, shell, horns, or skin.

predators (PREH-duh-terz) Animals that kill other animals for food.

protect (pruh-TEKT) To keep safe.

Index

A
Africa, 10, 14
alligators, 6, 10

B
bacteria, 13

C
carapace, 8
crabs, 6, 20
crocodiles, 6, 10, 13

D
defense, 6

E
exoskeletons, 16

F
feathers, 4

G
gastropods, 18

H
habitats, 4
hippo(s), 6, 13

L
lizards, 10
lobsters, 6, 20

M
mammal(s), 14
millipede, 13

P
pangolin, 14
plates, 6, 14, 16
predators, 6, 10, 22

S
scutes, 8, 14
shell(s), 4, 6, 8, 10, 13,
    18, 20
skin, 4, 6, 10, 13, 16
snakes, 10

T
tail, 10

W
water, 8, 13, 20

Web Sites

Due to the changing nature of Internet links, PowerKids Press has developed an online list of Web sites related to the subject of this book. This site is updated regularly. Please use this link to access the list:

www.powerkidslinks.com/cnature/armor/